Saturnine

Saturnine

poems by

Grace Rodriguez

Copyright © 2024 by Grace Rodriguez

All rights reserved. This book (or any part thereof) may not be reproduced or used in any manner without prior written permission of the publisher, except for brief quotations in critical articles or reviews.

ISBN: 979-8-218-45773-0

The world is a lonely place; it clamors for attention, so let us amplify its whispers.

Contents

Preface....1

Ambidextrous...5
Apparition...7
Trivialized Symphonies....9
Where I'm from....11
Anger II....13
Nonpareil....15
Medusoid....17
The Birds Ate the Moon....19
Nemesis....21
Solipsist's Ode to Sequence....24
Hint of Spring....26
Chapel of Torment....28
Frostbite....30
Overture....32
Svelte and Comely....34
Empaths Burn....36
Demeter....38
Acquiescence....40
Hunger and Thirst....41
Womanhood....42
The Girls....44
Altruism....46
Vainglorious....48
Regalia....50
Father....52

Fog Advisory....54
Transient Tourist....56
Fragmentary Understanding....58
The Arsonist and the Anarchist....60
Penumbra....62
Saturnine....64
Radicalized....66
Pandemonium....68
Vernal Equinox....69
Stigma and Dogma....71
Déjà Vu....73
Dread and Adage....75
Palindrome and Cult....77
The Dirge of the Actias Luna....79
The End....80

Interlude....82

Revelation....84
Primal....86
Secretive History....88
Bisan....90
Mother....92
Death by Guilt....94
An Open Letter to Gaza....96
Resistance....98
The Children Haunt Me....100
The Human Experience....102
Old Pain....104
Nakba....106

Preface

Let's talk about feelings, shall we? I think there is a lot of stigma around our capacity to confront such stirrings. I guess it is an odd concept—
the emotions that consume us like tidal surges—and we find ourselves immersed in raw sensation. Sometimes we are unaware; sometimes it happens against our will, but ultimately, we all experience them. Feelings are the essence of our human disposition, shaping our perceptions, decisions, and interactions with the world around us. These invisible threads weave through the fabric of our lives, whether it be negative or positive; we confront them head-on.

For me, being in tune with my inner self is intrinsically strenuous. It requires lengthy navigation because I tend to opt for neglect. So, I won't pretend like I'm an expert on the matter. All that to say, I simply wish to encourage others to rely on the manifestation of said emotions, to be privy to one's innermost thoughts and welcome the inevitable.

Saturnine encompasses all the below: every interminable aspect of the emotional realm. For example…

Joy is a sweet embrace from within— the laughter that bubbles up uncontrollably, the smiles that spread across our faces like sunshine breaking through clouds. Though it can be fleeting, it is always comforting.

Sadness is a heavy rain that washes over us, soaking us with a mix of sorrow and reflection. It's the tears that flow silently, the heaviness in our chest that weighs us down. Sadness teaches us about loss and failure, leading to moments of introspection and growth.

Anger is a fiery force that ignites within us, fueling passion and intensity. It can be irrational at times, but for the most part, it's the adrenaline rush that propels us into action, the sharp words that cut through the air. Anger shows us our boundaries, pushing us to stand up for ourselves and demand attention to what matters most to us.

Fear is a whisper in the dark— a primal instinct that keeps us alert and cautious. It's the racing heart, the sweaty palms, the quickened breaths. Fear can be paralyzing; it reminds us of our vulnerability, but also of our strength to overcome challenges and protect what we hold dear.

Love is the gentle melody that connects us to others in profound ways. It's the butterflies in our stomach, the warmth that spreads through our veins. Love restores our faith and teaches us about compassion and longing.

Empathy is the bridge from which we reach strangers and their condition. It is the driving force behind a more tolerant worldview because we are each other's most valuable resource. Empathy is a guide on our journey to becoming more benevolent individuals.

Saturnine is not a state of deficiency or gloom; it is the intangible residence of the sentient being that develops in the soul and settles in the cornea, so that those capable of feeling may also seek. It is an invitation to feel, which is, after all, what makes us undeniably human.

Let us not shy away from the richness of
our feelings—
they're all fleeting, momentary, anyway—
so, let yourself be carried away.

You won't drown, seriously, even if you
swear you will. Despite every hurdle, you
are sentient, still prevailing, a winding story
in prose. Your resilience is ever so evident,
even in the dimmest of rooms.

Ambidextrous

Allow me to set the scene:
It's 7:50 AM; I've slept a measly few
hours, but I think I've woken up on the
right foot.
The bathroom is unoccupied,
and I actually have an appetite.
I look through the blinds and witness the
overcast—
The sky is weeping, mirroring my disdain
for proactive conversation.
By this point, my throat is already drying
up.

The guiltless morning makes me question
if I'm in pain or just emotionally drained.
If it's the Monday blues or the inopportune
hook drilling my noggin.
Everyone else seems to be on cloud nine,
choking on compliments.
I want to tell them I'm ambidextrous,
but deep down I know I'll always be left-
handed—
meaning I am not capable of exhibiting
benevolent symmetry or adopting a benign
mindset.

My melancholy is boiling inside me,
like a stew in a cauldron,
yet I can only think as far as breakfast takes me.

It's 9:15 AM, and I'm palpably agonizing,
as if the worst is yet to come.
Discreetly losing track of time until I clock out,
forcing myself to transcend with vertigo
and grace.

I am no good at human interaction,
yet for some reason unbeknownst to me, I was hired to speak—
to relay words of affirmation to novice ears,
subliminal messages that target the right audience.
And once again, I plead innocence.

Apparition

Did the tendrils of verve probe your wound
as it began to scab?
Honestly, did they brook no opprobrium?

While writing of dreams and
conceptualizing hallucinations,
did they twine around your delusions
and slash your innards
to reveal the carrions flensing the rind?

That is the price of all creation.
To compose a single prose
is to kill plenty.

In seclusion, we learn to spot cavities
like symptoms of pestilence,
to pluck any fault like a sign of tedium.

To be spineless and sophisticated,
yet always starved.

To hoist the mantle and ferment your
incense until it seethes like some hot
reviving brew.

To see the apparition in a mirage
and mask the scent of all the ghosts
reaching out to possess you.

That is precisely how we become
invertebrate—
distorted and fecund—
so that we may create chaos in linear form.

Trivialized Symphonies

I crave not to build meaningful
relationships
or mend the fissure between sectors,
but to escape the auric vibrations carried by
them.

You call it a rift in friendship,
and I must say you've cracked the code.

My platform feels unstable,
and I wish to disparage everything and
everyone
until my waspish tongue is stunned—
to mitigate this rendition of coexistence,
and call it what it really is:
a pain in the ass.

But try as I might to run,
I am tormented by hellos,
trivialized symphonies I intend to dispose
of.

A reciprocal factor,
glorified interaction between rag doll and
scarecrow,
with cubic cerebrum and plaited bodice.

Charred body outlines on my front lawn
of all the people I've cut off without reason.

Avert my hasty honesty,
my vital fidelity.

I roll the dice,
tenants of addled mind
basking under the melting sun in an
ungainly sprawl,
in the guise of impunity.

You see, I am culpable too.
I must be held responsible
for putting up a wall impossible for anyone
to climb.

Pinkish angst undertone,
labial quivering, and spicy gossip,
sealing the vermillion.

Border of nonsense—my burden to digest.
Delve into my solvent loneliness once
again,
kiss my oral commissure farewell.

Where I'm from

When they ask me where I'm from,
I'm at the beach; my toes buried in the sand.
I am crouched on shallow waters,
hands wafting through the currents,
looking for hermit crabs in the submerged rocks.
I am advocating for the urchins and the whelks,
collecting scallops and conches.
I am of the sea, despite not knowing how to swim; climbing the crags is where you'll find me,
hoping the waves don't subdue.

When they ask me where I'm from,
I'm lost in the expanse—in the acres of grasslands.
I'm enthralled by the multitude of thyme and rues,
bearing harmonious nectar, contending with the firmament; the rain precipitates and the ladybugs must migrate.

When they ask me where I'm from,
I'm on the terrace, chomping on
pumarosas;
the carambola is chopped into stars,
and the plank smells of abundance.

When they ask me where I'm from,
the goosebumps come unbidden,
never tardy or slackening.
The unremitting drizzle flustering the
foreign Sahara dust,
the rooster crows,
the Maga flower is swooning over the
wired fence.

When they ask me where I'm from,
a coquí in Borikén vocalizes
how much of a traitor I am.

Anger II

The prodigies made a foray against the
occultists;
Ergo, they were of pagan descent—
subhuman,
if one's to speculate.
Indigenous invaders, first of their sort;
a garrison mustered on the verb,
for the noun is pervasive.
Which is to say, they are less than.

To be remotely cognizant of the cacophony
of chaos
is to be adrift—
to allow the anger that surges like a tempest
within
to settle.

In the visceral struggle,
where the very fabric of composure
unravels,
leaving behind a poignant residue of
despair.

The throes that probe my temper,
when patience proves no longer guidance.

Clamoring for the resistance
on which our reasoning is predicated,
to lash out at the anchor that remains
elusive.

Forbearance ignites timidity;
it begets the ease with which men
hobble towards the drop.

Let my aggravation ring forth from the
lofty mountaintops,
because, whether I like it or not,
my spattering mouth begins to spill out
words I must hold myself accountable for.

Nonpareil

In the calm of morning,
I count myself lucky to dawdle over coffee,
as the lazurite sky softens,
tamed by the sun that kindles its gastric
pool a variegated indigo,
melting the nautical dusk,
to unearth its tenderness.

It is reclining with a cornucopia,
simply in repose,
like a swallowtail slouched against the
narcissi
before resuming her journey.

It is, in all its splendor,
ushering in the stillness of wispy clouds
above a riverbank festooned with marsh
marigolds.
Algae and lichen on the bark of the willow
bush,
the trout striving for a leap of faith.
It reminds me that nature's creation is
inimitable.

She is a nonpareil artisan,
molding a paradisal Elysium.
Image and likeness, old and true.

And so, I tell her:
String me along, I dare you.
All that is will continue to be.

I embrace the ventral vignette widening—
The owl hooting atop the alder,
it is nice to be acquainted.

Medusoid

Someone spit out a nib
that prickled my frontal lobe;
now my inkling impulsivities
are tenoned into oracular runes
that portend ill omens.

Mortal creeds inferred from iniquitous truths—
This archetype of a medusoid
attempts to agglutinate one way or another,
whether today or tomorrow,
to satisfy his weird brother.

Its unsegmented body means to subsume life
and govern the pith of all its existence.
There's consistency in his vision,
a noble stag he may not be,
but he conveys his message quite clearly.

In the tidal mouth,
the estuary where the river meets the sea,
this gelatinous creature mortifies the leviathan.
Adding emphasis to the magnification.

The wheels of fortune are fast turning,
and its vicissitudes must continue evolving.

There's a strange gale coming,
chilling this village before the summer's end.
The slight undulation will unmask the rocketeer—
nematocysts; a paradigm for mockery.
Oh, the irony!
Do not hesitate to pretend
like you did not see it approaching.

The Birds Ate the Moon

It was a frigid night
when the moon fell from its hook
and dangled crookedly from the sky's
paunch.
Crescent as it was—screaming for the white
dwarf to fuse,
it became a waning smile.

Waxing in its axis,
plucking the stars that took the brunt of it.
She stalked the shadow away,
shook with mirth in solitary drunkenness,
and the sun came in a wonted flare,
bringing forth the ravenous crows.

The sparrow stood vigil, awaiting its turn,
as the aviary burst suddenly,
and the pecking commenced,
shrouding the lunar orb we once doted on,
so that none would behold this dame.

The scientists say the birds ate the moon
and left no trace of her—
no remains of its iridescent flesh
for the human hand to capture.

Lost in its stardom,
in desultory fashion,
the heavens mourned this cosmic disarray.
Rupture is in the stature of every celestial being,
living vicariously through the interstices of the sternum,
with a hand in its esophagus, destined to fester.

Nemesis

I often find myself wondering
whether I'm sound or sane,
always right or craftily vain.
Whether I'm the director or the protagonist,
I think I'm neither—
or rather, the ladder.

I assimilate the agony,
the tears, the rapture,
but I don't think anyone's collided with the
devil just yet,
or given a performance worthy of praise.

I don't think I'm as hollow as you say;
I'd argue everyone's logic is flawed,
and I'm as mellow as the world lets me.

Despite my so-called narcissistic
tendencies,
I value strategy over quantum
compensation,
novelty over wanton rectitude.

I am not callous or abrasive,
but I do tend to be impassive and reticent.

We are playing a game you can't win,
but I'll surely ace;
that way, you can divert the blame,
assign it to whoever's quieter,
and file a claim with the higher-ups
to vilify them.

A precarious labyrinth
that leads you to a somber place
where you writhe in pain,
regurgitating allegations,
throwing around insults like sobriquets.

I wear your labels like a badge of
attainment,
implicating I am the culprit.

I'd say I feel almost guilty,
but maybe I'm deflecting in a deadpan
tone—
a laconic response to your pruned morse
code.

The assertion that I'm your paralysis demon
is a loosely based premonition,
a tale as old as time;
the tint and hue of your perfect crime,
a sequence of multitudinous deeds
that make you a petty nemesis.

Solipsist's Ode to Sequence

I always miss it when it's gone,
the pungent ambience of reality.
When I walk alone, traversing
the slough of misery imposed upon me,
I am once again expected to show restraint.

A much wiser person would attest
that I have a flair for escapism—
(not to be mistaken with procrastination).
I no longer linger in squalor,
oscillating about my lowest point like a hammock.
I'd rather muse on fallacies unlikely to happen.

Once I'm stuck in a rut,
the mythos dissipates my hysteria.
I start to idealize my purpose,
led by stirrings of fervor,
in order to bypass the block—
much like falling in reverse.

A vague analogy to vouch
that you will learn the solipsist's ode to
sequence, eventually;
to be routinely blunt
and take no umbrage at the suggestion of
camaraderie.
The two can coexist, I think;
we can be reflexively cordial, you and me.

Hint of Spring

I am mire and fungus, limestone and eve;
perennial and sedimentary.
Retching homesick outburst,
appalling winter boots,
I lead the body with the shoes.

In a nightmare of naked trees,
I open my eyes and see no foliage trilling
underfoot.
I was born in April,
which makes me a hint of spring—
unable to play model minority,
although I could just be a red herring.

A sudden gush of vitriol within season,
seamless avoidant attachment under false
pretenses.
I slide through the crevices of my gripping
hope,
from the multitude of ambitions I've let go.
I convert everything that's good into foe,
into arms and gear.

I hold onto my fear,
press it tight against my chest,
apply pressure where it hurts best.

To collude and connive at my own
escapade.

I am impervious to your saliva,
to your overbearing temper,
your overflowing feelings spilling.
You take up too much space for me to
tolerate
what I no longer find beneficial.

Yet, I show no disdain.
Aries refrains from rising to the bait.

Chapel of Torment

I met a jester in a cathedral,
praying for deliverance—
or perhaps a stroke of fortune.
He wished to become an apothecary in his
father's stead,
but what man can conjure up delusions at
his wit's end?

He did not believe in medicine,
for what anodyne could soothe the clangor
in his abdomen?
So, he resorted to antics and debauchery,
until the harlequin came along to thwart his
plans.

Thanks to reformation,
and not the odds of favor,
they were sealed away together in this
chapel of torment.
The echoing of bells, the only melody
amidst the chaos,
overblown with the taste of geniality—
led by sympathy and the sourness of
amenity,
they forgot to proceed with equanimity.

Here, their chains became jewelry
made from the finest of stones.
This place is vast and taunting,
but oh, they understand it so well,
and I'm afraid to admit they might have
come to render it free.
Spate of auguries achieved;
every sinew of their twisted bodies
bows before this shrine.

Frostbite

In my instance of affliction,
the moment my reckoning commenced,
a thought struck me—
like a tornado swirling about the
opposition.

It was a conjecture
that led me to spiral into coherence,
and suddenly, my words started making
sense.

You were obsessing over boys with fragile
masculinity,
so naturally, the prologue was skipped.
The rebuttal was a sickle to my head;
you delivered it flawlessly,
but if you wanted me dead,
you could've just said so.

I am unsure whether it is caprice or a
hunch,
but I think I was meant to reincarnate as a
prayer.
Hyper-fixation aside, I am invisible,
so, I might as well turn to religion.

If someone calls out my name with
credence,
will I matter then?
That was an innocuous question;
do not stint yourself.

Perhaps I am loved after all,
in a certainly ambiguous way.
Maybe I have an ounce of wisdom to
contribute.

I see the steady cracking of snow;
frostbite and afterdrop.
A feeling of avoidance packed a hefty
punch,
and I was overtaken by a whim.

It was a lovely dream indeed,
and this time,
I was asleep to witness it.

Overture

Under the guise of singularity,
we ponder the overture of our autonomy.
In the simulacrum of temporal decay,
was there ever an instance of finesse?
This odyssey we deem salutary is a clear
indication of a disequilibrium that
dispossesses us of all merit.

That is, to certify the premise of our
findings—
the prelude of a sanctitude forthcoming.

What a predicament we find ourselves in:
three words, a stress-relieving curse
followed by a pound to the human psyche.

There are whimsical stories to narrate,
after we determine how much anecdotes are
worth in actuality,
like a dowry in a patrilineal society.

Errant aisles a mime did wend before they
lost their way.

Your atlas is the gift of temperance;
it'll lead you out of purgatory so you may
edify your emaciated spirit,
until it transmutes into someone
magnanimous and resplendent.

Svelte and Comely

Rake my feet; plow my ovaries,
you'll garner detritus and mulch.
Leave me here in this humid shelter,
where the sprinklers drench me with
nitrogen juices—
I'll rot before I satiate my lack.

You'll cut the furrow in my soil
and harvest nothing of value.
I exhort you to look elsewhere,
though if you insist, scuff the heel of your
shoe
before you enter my sanctum at least.

I give; you take.
I remain on the losing end of the table,
raffling off scraps so you'll spare me.
A fair exchange, you say—
unsolicited, but equitable, nonetheless.

I heave the burden back into place
until I decay,
spoil my potential
so you can muster up your courage
and whip me into shape.

Do try your best;
the brusque spout of hostility
always does the trick.
I choke on dirt and debris,
swallow your words as a remedy.

You guarantee I'll grow svelte and comely
if I lie bare before you,
and I admit, this fine evening
you sound more convincing than yesterday.

Empaths Burn

When your tongue splits
and disintegrates into tiny particles,
in a sheet of searing blaze,
look at the rapids—
their expansion,
the eddies that stem in a flat plane,
raked by the battered wind;
the airflows that strike the coniferous.

Does your environment startle you?
The robust entitlement that belies its depth?

When your tenor shrinks,
becomes less than a minor function,
and does not inflect a thing,
do not speak.
Loose lips sink ships,
so, it is best to mute yourself,
lest your words veer into an arc.

I have come to realize
that empaths burn like luminaries—
unhurriedly, pacing, as some candid spirit.
Whorled and concentric,
to seem blither than the common melodist.

It takes pleasure in the mundane,
as if it were a great discovery.

Oh, cruel fate,
that binds us in such ties,
to feel the world's woes.

The stale pallor of normality,
interspersed between expressions of forfeiture
and jests supplying comic relief,
turns into something overbearing,
spoiled to its core—
and it withers so.

Occasionally, you appeal to the conscience
of the watcher on the walls;
going round in circles,
he slips into an oath of desperation.

Demeter

She is the sacred flame
that wavers in the draft,
a flaring luminance
that flickers and falters before one's eyes.
As she mourns,
she allows the earth to shrivel up for a time,
embracing the barrenness
known as winter.

Demeter loves no one more than
Persephone,
so, when the cold comes screeching and
scathing,
resurrected by the motivation
to immortalize her grief with the
immediacy of penalty—
blame Hades.

For the permanent bruise of devastation
channeled into the avalanche,
nipped in the bud,
until it became a canopied bed in a tuft of
grey hairs.

Drapes of persuasion
bring forth the primrose that greets the azalea,
makes way for the bulbous daffodil
and paints the hyacinth a bluish mauve.

Acquiescence

Splinter my hands so they won't ask for more—
rip them apart, shatter them in four.
Make them go rigid, so I don't have to feed them anymore.

They are never quite acquiescent,
refusing to weave into each other; they unravel instead.
They expect too much, which always hurts,
because some days there isn't much to offer.

Ooze them out, make them weep.
Maybe then they'll go silent.
Hold them loosely, but more dearly.
Make them settle down for once.

Hunger and Thirst

If I politely asked you to kiss my poisoned lips,
would you do as I say?
Softly, slowly, drink the wine away?
Tackle me down with your serene touch,
whisper in my ear you'll drain me completely.

I don't ask for much:
pluck my soul until it aches,
swallow me wholeheartedly,
fill my eyes with gloss until they flood with shimmer.

There's nothing I would rather see
than your body howling at the sun in incandescent thrill,
your damp hands nipping at my waistline,
digging through my torso with intensity.

Eat my fear away,
cut its strings and bring me back to life.
Make my ego shrivel,
undo my hunger—awake my thirst.

Womanhood

Womanhood is unerring divinity,
an integral wonder in the bleakest of
spheres.
The cogency of course in a ruinous path,
a promise of excellence, the soundness of
reason throughout history.

Womanhood is perseverance,
a beacon of agency against obscurity.
It is the mightiest stronghold,
a steadfast fortress built to withstand any
number of odds,
a song composed by our mothers,
to be heard through the epochs of feminism.

As beautiful and full of mist as a siren,
it is the poised hymn that will never be
silenced.

And so, I dismantle the coffer the
goddesses were sealed away in,
carve a waxen crest as an insignia of
success to commemorate them.

Venus, bless me.
Aphrodite, preside over our trials.

Hera, allow us to replete with valor and eminence in the face of adversity.
Athena, gauge our intrinsic legacy.
Artemis, I hope not to be one among the few, but the many.

The Girls

This is for the girls who keep quiet and still
expect to be heard,
the girls who chew their lip before they
speak, anxiously awaiting their turn,
the girls who spend too much time
daydreaming,
the girls with the metallic façade and wiry
frame,
who live between the crevice of solidity
and intricacy;
seeking refuge from the rain under torn,
frayed tents—but to no avail.
Hail is already descending upon them,
and granite is licking hard at their skin.

I know you stand in the corner of the room,
biting nails as you utter your first words,
your teeth becoming bloody with each one.
And a man whispers from your rear:
"You'd look prettier if you smiled!"

It's no big surprise you shift and shed your
armor.
You swallow the mildew yet show no sign
of discoloration.

Things will get better, sister.
If I lie, pull me by the tresses and call me a deceiver.
Nevertheless, I hope the impotency does not linger for much longer—
we still have a world to conquer.

Altruism

My nightmares are usually cold-livered,
vivid affairs that propel me to look inward,
as if mirroring my covert egotism.
I'm scythed at shifting intervals,
wavered in masked altruism.

These possessions are gruff and ripple,
indisputably lethal.
They smother me with plans to plunge
headfirst into the water,
only to drift downstream,
to sink as deep as my wizened lungs will let
me and emerge sovereign.

Perhaps if I had been pampered from a
young age,
these infant fantasies would forsake me;
I'd be confined to business acumen
instead of inane artifices and citrous antics.
I would have a flair for enterprises
instead of dramatic essays.

If my depression enabled me to pivot,
to kick the bucket, to scamper in like a
dashing rodent,
I would be released from this torment.

I would feel something other than
carnivorous nothing.

They say misery loves company,
but I'd rather be alone and forlorn,
tossed into a dungeon in a fore-and-aft
motion.
I think I would feel elated
if I could see the omens in my steaming
entrails
melt away with ease.

I think I would finally feel at peace
if I could resort to violence like intermittent
fasting,
bench-press the dead weight I've been
clasping while multitasking.
I would delve in solitude,
perforate your eardrum with the potency of
quietude.
You'd be overcome by lassitude,
and I'd be saluted with sincere gratitude.

Vainglorious

I'm caught in a skirmish every instant;
I grow greener, more stubborn, yet never
quite ripe—
swivel-eyed and uptight,
fixated on a fleeting delight roving through
the timeline,
bringing no insight to my life.

I am a coil of sunshine, sweltering out of
spite,
gathering courage to succeed
in a graveyard
ready for the burial of my withered dreams,
living on flaunted luxury and maniacal
schemes.

When my anxiety meets my entitlement,
turpitude takes center stage;
I appeal to the vacuous silence,
but my vices know not to disengage.

They blur the lines in thresholds,
unbothered by lectures of conceit and
vainglorious deeds—
unfettered chambers of false hope.

The nexus between covert elation and lamentable ohs,
my deplorable lows.

The flimsy lows of adulthood are stealthy ghosts in spandex,
ravenous permutations of failed alliances that deter me from growing.

Regalia

Who is she?
An imperious embrace, lost in reverie—
a note of levity in the gilded omphalos
of a historical composition, hinting at
vulgarity.
A galling Gordian knot of some sort, I'm
guessing—
the twinge in the wing that burrows deeper
into the breast,
until it breaches the hawk's heart
and turns it a widowed black.

The monsoon season that fetes
the meniscus enervation,
foreshadowing severance.
She is a ludicrous essence,
epoxied to a fable;
a fossilized treatise,
desiccated bestiary bound to devour you—
a divine regalia swathed in velvet satin.

Royalty, destitute of arrogance,
too dour to appear nude.

With your regal scepter, you'll sit
on your perverse throne,
only to be wrung out of all armature.
You'd better not contest her;
it is in her nature to swerve
toward the opposite direction,
yet still arrive at that singular destination.

Father

Father is steam,
hot at the neck,
breaking down each layer of skin
like a microbial disease;
a pathogen derivative of affection
and moralizing acclamation.

Father is a spitting venom
leaking from the thorax,
strewn all over the church altar.

At 12 PM, the sermon ends,
and the flogging begins.

Father is the eternal question:
How can one feel so wayward
despite commodity and creed?

If I sound reproachful,
know I am not trying to be.

Paternity is revulsion
at the sound of echoing,
a bond that cuts.

The blistering heat of hibernation
that yawns the daughter bolt upright
from the nightmare.

He's not gone,
though I deliver this eulogy
as if he was.

Quite the avocation,
with many quirks;
cinematic, imaginary character.

Father is a term of endearment,
and that is to say
I am predisposed to love him.

Fog Advisory

The days are lethargic—
auspicious blank spaces
sketched absentmindedly,
abridged riddles
in scribbled handwriting.

Everyone is forced
to go to college
because talent is bought
if we enroll in the same curriculum.

Abilities are attained
through intricate exams
that test how much we are worth
in the real world—
a peculiar way to say
we're all the same.

There is no such thing as aptitude,
when they said dreams were just dreams,
consecutively
and soundly,
(but support is visible
somewhere amidst the fog advisory).

The poet is no valedictorian,
nor do they score summa cum laude.
Their existence is more of a holistic,
asinine limerick.

Uptown funk,
on a slightly high note…

It is a mesmerizing thing,
to be alive
against one's will.

More than unjust,
it is merciful,
to revolt and reboot,
until you can hear
the salving auroras
rushing to the cause.

Transient Tourist

Island breezes chime,
Taíno spirits murmur—
sun-kissed waves embrace.

I wrote a haiku in June,
under the neighboring birch.
Not a maple, not a half-truth.
How foolish to think I'd see Eden—
a pacific abode, somewhere other
than mowing the plot on a Tuesday.

Effeminate aficionados of the hunt;
they profane for sport,
commuting from Eucharist to Jim Crow.
Segregation and ultimatums—
how low can one go?
To desecrate all that is good,
and foment discord in the reserves
you lucratively conferred on the firstborn.

The cicadas do not drone for you;
the horizon is already filled to the brim
with inhibition,
intruding memories of effete contingencies.

We were one back then, ish,
an orographic fold challenging the gusts—
remember, ghostly traveler?

Despite your absence—
transient tourist, with your tranquil gaze—
the onus is on you
to answer for your duplicity
or be censured for your consent.

Fragmentary Understanding

Trails made of corn and salt
lead into the coppice where no herbage
grows at all.
Palms contemplate the ocean, to and fro,
prostrated in the distance,
splashed on dry soil and vacant terrain—
a fragmentary understanding that the world
isn't as vast as we think.

Datum counsels the unknown,
warranting that some secrets
will never reach the surface—
rather convenient for the indolent dog.

I see plainly the wealth you hoarded
in the foreword of sloth.
Now you pore over the bail to conserve
your indignation,
more of a symbolic gesture than anything
else.

Recluse patron of sores,
proverbial for your cunning,
you must have found your niche.

Silly fox,
insinuate you were duped into your
draconian laws—
that you never meant to become what you
are.
Then the discrepancy in each rapport will
be forgiven,
back to perfidy and panache.

The Arsonist and the Anarchist

To write is to lie.
Vulnerability comes hand in hand with delirium—
to pretend that you are talking to someone other than your subconscious
and projection; to attribute outside variables for your own defects.

There is little one can determine from the crossword of a moral absolutist,
and so, I give myself wholly to sensation.

There have been many occasions where I have been denuded of all inspiration,
hence why I try so little to be seen.

Where to begin?
Frankly, if I had to choose between laziness and excellence,
would I have the right to exceed my own expectations?

My words may just be the syntax of an unspoken language,
but they must invoke some instinct.

I elude my fatigues by spewing blather over affairs,
because I have always been a liar and a writer,
camouflaged with intent.

I am both the arsonist and the anarchist,
gauche about authority,
incendiary as a lewd adieu.

My thesis rewilds the ardor; it promulgates political dissonance.

Penumbra

I saunter into the mossed track,
bristled with spores,
and see a horde of stalked capsules rising
before me,
carpeting the asphalt.

A metamorphic cul-de-sac briefs me with
dare;
the wrens must've followed me here,
in search of the marquee.

The nuances of passerine behavior—
it confuses us all.
So much for the ephemeral beauty,
teeming with wildlife,
hovering beside the bumblebees foraging in
the uncut grass of my backyard.

There dwells a mythical nidus of
intricacies—
tussock, pale, and green;
the pea-sized bulb whispers inconceivable
secrecies to the deciduous elm.

The oriole, with its tourmaline plumage,
dances around a penumbra of uncertainty.

We have encountered the fastidious
shadow,
where the oasis of our serenity finds abode,
untrimmed as fern, yarrow, chicory…
You get the gist.

Saturnine

You are a specter ensnared in your
unfettered pocket dimension,
defeated by the gravitational pull of
cowardice.
Must you assuage your ideals and become
bereft of expectancy?
A sturdy aspen in poise, coalesced into the
annals of submission,
with coarsely toothed leaves fluttering in
even a slight breeze.

Is this your pursuit of peace?
To not defy the saturnine, but rather faint,
smelting in the furnace of comfort?

Solstice will not be kind to you, my friend.
This time, you will not regenerate from
sprouts
until you shed,
or face the threat of being hauled off to the
nursery again,
to be absorbed by the shade.

I am no botanist,
but I can tell you that none can survive in
this landscape.

You are no different,
sepulchered in this repellent setting,
privy to one's innermost thoughts.

Funny, is it not?
How the hoax exacerbates drought when
you are incapable of feeling.

All things considered,
this delights me not,
but to wave all worry, one must exhaust
every qualm.

Radicalized

It all started with the donkey and the elephant—
cartoonish crooks, apostates of the sect,
and colonists that arrived centuries after the Crusades.

Then came the imbecilic thugs in ties,
zeros to the left,
(inconsequential for obvious mathematical reasons).

Detestable speeches, and then some—
some Karen, with her face sallow and pitted,
will whine about being radicalized.

Verily, we are in the trenches,
Biblically accurate end times,
with the pharisees and the pharaohs,
not to mention the gluttonous tax collectors.

"Ironclad"—I've come to loathe that word;
it means unequivocal support.

The executioner pretends to be harrowed by hypotheticals.

I despise his wheezing,
reedy as an accordion's timbre.
The slurring mendacity distracting from his
blatant hypocrisy.

No red lines: he feigns dissent.

The other one, always tepid and seething,
for he is no psalmist—
he knows nothing about Corinthians.

Slathered on saffron, with a severe lack
of opulence and heresy in practice.

Hip to hip, accrete,
hedging bipartisan ethos of nationalism
and provocative fearmongering—
We are clearly not sending our best.

Pandemonium

The buzzing has intensified—
too boisterous now, in contrast to the hum.
The townsfolk thought nothing odd of
the month that began inordinately brisk and blustery,
yowling like some rabid beast, agitated in its enclosure.
People become accustomed to such tumult;
the nebulous babel of their confinement
makes up for the undesired silence.
Bedlam in an oubliette of their own designing—
is it the human tendency to be validated?
Humility does not blare, nor does it beg to be announced
through the bars like some clandestine visitor,
coeval with the menacing creature.
In this man-made pandemonium, slumber is doled out to us all.
Though you are drifting towards nirvana,
know the archangel fled the moment you poked the hornet's nest.

Vernal Equinox

Cygnet, bloom without me;
present yourself with the cherry blossoms
in the vernal equinox,
as shawls of lace twine around
in the dewy renewal.
Arrive nodding in golden clusters,
as spores of a dandelion scattered
across the meadow near the creek:
small, mystique, and make-believe.
Rise out of the pastoral browse
as a pretty swan, fair or suave—
be anything you want.

I will be ready too, eventually,
to join you.
We can congregate then,
glide gracefully through the opalescent
reservoir,
coaxed into a rendezvous.
I have not managed to morph yet—
I've stayed in the suckling stage,
procrastinating in my feather bed,
haloed in mist.
I am impersonating the dawn,
encircling the margin of caution,
trusting evolution will work its magic.

If you care to wait a little while
so that I can mimic your stride,
we will waddle—slender and synchronized,
reflecting on the Tiffany glass—
mature at last.

Stigma and Dogma

Goodness is tragedy unfolding,
as an unhinged sense of rhetorical clarity.
Poetic justice: the novelist recounts the plot
through aphorism and memoir, withholding
no certitude,
much to the consternation of the avid
observer,
who cares not to read the annotations
distilled into the book.

The tome bears no livelihood in the
corridors of greed—
words compiled from brazen minds and
forked tongues.
Between solemn cups and carpus cramps,
their alienation is duly noted.
Hollowed ignominy preaches something
different entirely;
staunch supporters uphold their eerie
desires, fermented in its pages.

What was once so benevolent a dispenser
of probity—
a paragon of virtue—has turned into an
insidious campaign,
rapidly escalating.

Transgressions and manifestations of pseudo-optimism,
inflicted by the frolics of a heretic.
The pith of such chronicle is plainly fictitious—
a pariah of many premises, inferred from stigma and dogma.

Déjà Vu

There is someone settling in the suburbs as we speak,
currently on their balcony, astonished by déjà vu—
memory anomalies when the neurons misfire,
or is it the split perception?
No matter; they won't stay for long.
It is all just a fractured seam, a tectonic shift—
bizarre chronology that can easily be blinked away.

Love is one of them;
it is not concise but sensible—
like the ventriloquist lunatic that controls you.
Your words are not your own,
just because they tug at your limbic system.
A prescient loop of emotional strings,
nodes like fists that lead to aching traffic.

Infatuation is the ultimate apex predator;
it is our mere instinct to want to abscond
with the heart we lent in an impetus.

Drive away, accelerate before regret seeps in.
Amygdala: the ride does not begin until the hippocampus opts in.

Dread and Adage

I yearned for you as any loner yearns for company,
secretly praying the misanthropy away.
I desired you discreetly, amidst the lust and the wiles—
neither driven nor beguiled into rife fornication or cursory pleasures.
Between the dread and adage, I craved every bit of you;
longed for your scanty fragrance that never stays,
the tartness of your pomatum that still travels through my garden—
risen from the soil and carried by the wind.

I revered your reluctance to concede
and the gap between your teeth,
your sonorous flatteries over emptied promises;
stricken by your indifference like some devoid trinket.
Not caring where it would get me, vagrant or smitten.

Laid to rest, agog to meet the tumulus,
with a kiss that mounds the prairie—
an embrace that assimilated into the fauna
and flora.

Palindrome and Cult

When the crippled find themselves
disoriented
by brooding threnody,
they become susceptible to social isolation
and minatory contradictions.
Burnt out of their minds,
they relinquish their uniqueness—
espouse the tunic and menial labor.

Deified: a word that twists and bends, then
sighs.
What symmetry it holds; feel the tale twice
told.
Similar frequencies assembling like cultural
rites.

Civic: the lonesome is prone to the tenuous
link,
snared by messianic kinks.
Palindrome and cult;
no matter which side you inspect it from,
it spells out the same doling malady.

The colossal mistake of confounding
catharsis with duty—
to be both judge and jury.

Indisposed and off the rocker, too.
Radar: I hope someone locates you.

This phenomenon is not an isolated incident,
but rather a deviant cycle of normality
that occurs as a souvenir of generational trauma.
We never learn our lesson;
instead, we carry on with the drama.

The Dirge of the Actias Luna

My poem is a song,
enjambed like the mind of the speaker—
rambling, eight days writing, and then drops dead.
My pen is a pistol, and my spasm pulls the trigger.
I run—you'll never catch me.

The dirge of the *Actias luna*;
moonlit sonnet I can't revise, flutters in a final trance.
Emerald sheen beneath the stars takes up nocturnal flight.
I must sleep, but the vestigial switch stays on.

The moth relies on energy it stored up as a caterpillar,
much like me, me…
Mediocre closing, beholden to the ink that flows with each strophe.
Redact the epistle; cue the critics.

The End

It is said that in the end, the world will be set ablaze,
and everything in it will be laid bare.
Hail and fire, mixed with blood, will be hurled down upon the earth,
and all life therein will be burned up—
a devastating reckoning that will bring about mayhem,
with a striking adagio to conclude.

No matter how many times the man hears the lecture,
he'll proceed at his own peril,
marching blindly toward his demise.
And he will perish along with the buildings, the skyscrapers,
and the weapons of mass destruction—
swiftly and of his own accord.

He will uplift the voice of the oppressor,
and ignore the plight and strife of the oppressed.

He will embrace apocryphal ideologies that
will not dispel inquiries,
hoping to banish the adversary prowling
around like a roaring lion,
seeking someone to devour.

He will hail the balm of anthems,
dabbing the secretion of a temporal
quiescence.
In the end, he will nourish his corporeal
yoke—
hoarse and strained through his arteries,
conveyed from the crudity of design to
oxygenate his callousness…
And these words will mean nothing to him.

Interlude

My beloved Palestine,

I wish to scoop you up from the rubble and hug you like no other; to bear your well of oath in my own ribcage, stoically, so that I never cease to fulfill my promise—to carry you with me to the grave. When the rivers stop flowing and the stars all fuse, when the deserts drown with snow, you will understand how much you mean to me.

I thank you because, before, I was consumed by numbness, incapable of expression. You have made me a better human being, and for that, I am incredibly grateful.

Palestine, I wish to adopt your sacred birthright like an orphan among the reeds, so that one day, when Palestinians return, they can wield it as a burning sword: for in the darkest nights, it remains theirs.

Palestine, you haunt me still, but I will stand by you in solidarity for eternity.

Know that I would recognize your offspring in a heartbeat—the olive trees, grafted onto Jesus, who is reflected in the eye of every one of your children; resilient and vigorous, dwelling in a land flowing with milk and honey.

The nation with many names, forever covered with the mantle of permanence. Colonized, occupied—no matter your creed or the language you speak, you have always been. I know this to be true, for God has revealed it, your history attests to your continuity. You are marked in my Bible as well as my soul, favored in perpetuity. I, too, bless thee.

Revelation

Freedom calls from the fringe of summation,
amidst plunder and liberation.
In the field of fire, with strings of flame and ire.

In remembrance—because the martyr is valiant,
and the soldier is craven.

Revolutionary is the tacit prophecy,
sung at the expense of the hungry and athirst.
A warning from above; the looming tyrant has woken by orisons,
and still the world rages on about throne and baton.

Measure your stance while there is ground to stand on.
Accusation is confession, void of introspection,
proclaiming itself victor.

It is the objective of our society to punish the victim.

Our champion is the orphan child
with candor and repudiation.

Bless his soul, bless his patience,
for he still heralds a revelation.
With anticipation, he dreams of broken shackles
and ushers a new prayer.

Every waking moment—with every fervid inhale
of hope and fumes intertwined,
spewed by thy neighbor.

Primal

I take to the apogee of my despair and
succumb to the rain,
soaking in the tears, summoning the
wind—to caress my sorrow,
swell my affliction, so that I may never
become complicit.
I carry my guilt like a conveyor of
clemency,
and as I implore God to intervene,
this somber evening, my eyes deceive me.
I see everything for what it's always been:
an odious gimmick,
a plethora of calumny and slander the
weary until they cannot fathom the abuse,
a perversion of all ordinances.

I am haunted by the image of the crippled
infant, mouth agape with incredulity—
she is premature once again, reduced to the
germinal stage.
Girl, what is your name? Where is your
mother? Has my country failed you?
I want to ask if my prayers have reached
her,
if my benignity has hindered the siege, if
only for a brief interlude.

The price of freedom is death,
but please, don't let it be her.

I am smothered by the idea of *Jannah*.
I was anointed with oil at the altar,
she was born into bane and havoc.
Her dress is fuchsia; mine was too,
except hers is soiled with blood and mine
with mud.

Thankfully, we move forward, toward
progress and purview.
Unfortunately for her, all this bleak world
has left her is terror.
How primal are we?
This earth is brimming with ash and bone.
Beware of the cadavers in your closet;
do not step on their prerogative to denounce
their own right to exist.

The civilized always win; with their tanks
of courtesy, they conquer the continent.
The patriots are adherent, the liberals at
ease—despotism is the language we are
most fluent in.
At the sight of penury, America prospers—
united as one.

Secretive History

The nomadic tribes now sojourn in the land
of the pyramids,
as opposed to the placid strip with the olive
groves.
Through the Kidron, exiled by the
malignant ones.
The sheikh, who was also a herder, scurried
to his tent
as assailants razed covenanted valleys with
bulldozers—
No consecration ceremony took place.

Fables of nativity prompt imperial
reckoning:
skeletal rattle and clement collisions,
some secretive history.
One must point out that the book on the
shelf
is indeed always repeating itself.

The usurper's barbarity knows no bounds;
it remains an indelible blot on the soul of
mankind.
Seventy-six years ago, they hacked off the
trees from their trunks,
but the veins remained.

Rejoice, imposters, with your spears and javelins,
the morrow steers the squadrons you will not overrun.

Bisan

Breathtaking—that's how one would describe her.
With coined shatweh and embroidered thobe,
the maiden looks upon the Dome of the Rock, wishing she, too, could ascend to heaven.
She is delicate like a poppy, native as the Iris haynei from Faqqu'a,
though she has never visited Jenin.

Lovely Bisan, you were named after the ancient city of light and deity.
The essence of your source preserves a heritage flecked with bronze, perfumed by the jasmine of the Levantines,
whence the ore is procured, and the elders convene.
Painted lady, you are impossible to forget—
genial and courageous beyond comparison and thence illuminating.

Hakawatya, how pleasant your retellings of
a bittersweet past,
of a Palestine that insists on giving,
yields its bounty, lush and homely,
endures and revives anew—a testament to
be—with asphodels draped in anguish, yet
still flourishing, just like you.

Mother

There is a mother in Rafah,
tearing her abaya to sew
the excess fabric into a blanket.
She cradles a corpse, believed to be her
only son,
declaring Allah has willed it.
Affliction is an echelon to the follower
who seldom stays there,
knowing it is a catalyst to the other side,
the entry into paradise.

The mother grips her hijab,
uncertain of when they should reunite.
The Mighty One will call into account
the tares among the wheat,
and she remembers the lullabies
she will never sing to a baby
whose teething had not yet begun.

Lamenting her inability
to wrench the windpipes from her throat,
she recites a Qur'anic verse.
The mother crawls from under the rubble
and finds herself in Yafa,
observing the Mediterranean coastline.

The tasbih beads have turned to shrapnel,
inured to harden with each salah,
barring her from dreaming,
transcending into the spiritual realm.
She is from Hebron,
but this is not Abraham's sanctuary;
here her kin find no approbation.

There is no hyperbole in this scenario;
safety is all but an illusion.
Her faith has been honed over generations,
remedied with conflation and disregard.
The mother remains steadfast amidst the exodus
and finds solace in the aquifers of Bethlehem.
She is no longer bound to the walls of Jericho,
but Nablus will never see her charm.

Death by Guilt

Damn my crimson vote and my settler
colonial income,
my impotence and, therefore, succor;
like the aberrant deed, collaboration abases
itself as good intention,
proselytizing the devotee.

I bow and scrape the basis of impartiality
as if it were the summit of objectivity,
the gap between conjecture and praxis,
the lasso tightening the neck of the abettor,
aiding the aggressor.

There is no treading carefully on the verge
of death by guilt;
you either yield or scream at the seams
until rebellion and mutiny give way to
peace.

Yet, I can't help but wonder: what happens
when we do not see?
My lungs are filled with vitriol and
repugnance;
I bite my tongue to prevent myself from
cursing.

I find the spawn no different than his
depraved forebears—
the personified continuation of injustice,
the foundation of aberration, an extension
of their malice.

The mason's tribulation is the minister's
interpretation of integrity;
no commandment holds greater weight than
his blasphemy,
casting aspersions, immune to all obloquy.

Perhaps I am blinded by aversion,
and I have no sympathy left to give.
Soul of my soul, a little girl named Reem—
Elohim, save Falasteen.

An Open Letter to Gaza

Greetings, to Whom It May Concern,
I'll skip the introduction,
for I am no one of importance.
I wish to confess, get it off my chest,
that I have failed you today.

I yearned for solace in my passivity,
equated my advocacy to exemption of
person.
I welcomed a partial repose,
had the temerity to give up,
dwelling in my sadness a little too long.

I know you don't have the agency to do as
much—
that the oppressor seized your jubilee—
yet I had the privilege to exert resistance
without impunity.
I sobbed myself to sleep,
and I woke up with my walls still standing,
my room intact, my drawers shut.

I know we are vastly different,
however much it hurts to verbalize.
Our differences imply that prejudice and
bigotry still thrive in our league.

I am a sentient being,
but I forget that, on closer inspection,
I prove to be negligent all the same.

I hope you find it in your heart to forgive me,
for I still wish to be your friend.
Thank you, Gaza, for showing me the way.
My sincerest apologies for my blunder and sway;
there is so much more I want to say,
but for now…
I extend this letter, signed with fondness and solidarity.

Resistance

Terrorists, ye who resist—
the machine must feed.
You ought to adhere to my commands;
keep your neck stiff under my boot
until I am satisfied.

Between rows of bunting and venial chants,
know endurance is frowned upon.
Quondam defiance, albeit suppressed, must
be ruthlessly eradicated.

I have redeemed your accounts,
claimed your ideas rooted in violence—
sown by vindication-as my own.
You should've surrendered when I flicked
my fingers,
before I loaded my gun.

Bear witness to the shrill of condemnation;
notice how it sounds a lot like fusillade.
Three seizures are an annual pilgrimage.
I am being prudent,
yet you overlook my kindness and oppose
this sacrament.

Your savagery must be supplanted
by my stipulation
so that this desert may flourish.

Stand down or I will shoot!
As a matter of fact, leave now;
this was never your home to begin with.

The log is caught in your lash, Ersatz
savant.
And to you I say:
this will not absolve you of your sins;
justice is calling.

The Children Haunt Me

The children haunt me, as though I extirpate
the fig of their youth before it develops anchorage.
They nag me, as though I deprive them of sap,
hindering their growth, as though I kill their dreams
and their hopes—plucking the stem and tertiary root
like only a fiend could.

They daunt me in a drunken stupor, these junipers,
as though I were an inebriate.
I did not raise my hand against them—
maybe my silence did.
The instances in which I parried the talons of the eagle,
turned a blind eye to the lines that encompassed morale.

The younglings resist persisting in growing;
I see them in tatreez and watermelon seeds.

Tonight, they come to visit me;
I wrap myself in my sheets as if they were
linen and gauze.
I will be mummified after being torn from
the inside,
perpetually repeating the same fractal
pattern.

My daughter and son;
I was a mature girl once,
now I am a childish woman,
condemned to expiate for the burning
shame
of not knowing your stories.

Please, forgive the adult in me,
for I, too, was a sapling once—
ecstatic at the prospect of aging.

The Human Experience

My love is primordial; it extends itself and transcends me,
singes the uterus, disrupts all convivial habits.
You cannot sever the connection.
We stretched our arms across continents,
like lanterns through the sand,
and we reached each other, locked hands.
A shared refrain, carved in the septum of our collective cry.

Strangers we were, but I swear your despair is my own—
abrasion that spurs empathy to swell like a requisite one is unable to quell.
I cannot contain the poignancy of the human experience,
thrusting a stake through the impenetrable.
It sends me adrift, whirring through the vacuous ether.

No risk of contagion; the resonance in the marrow solidifies,
as heady and patent as a vinous crash.

Nothing else takes precedence;
it was the fleck that flitted about the lachrymose
that culminated my inertia.
Now I am compelled into action;
my protest is a symbol of atonement.

Old Pain

Please return to me my defunct grief and
my farcical worries.
The old pain: acne and body.
Make me abstruse, as well as somnolent—
an esoteric, philosophical marionette
captivated by schematic stanza.

Lately, my mood has trespassed on
barricaded property,
and the pesky owner has alerted the
authorities.
Where do I go from here?
It is as if my circumstance fluctuates from
one side of the spectrum,
like my progenitors, though they would not
commiserate with my rude awakening.

Past misfortunes seem so nonsensical,
insignificant.
I still adopt the anaphora when it is
appropriate,
but now the machinery is obsolete.

I accept liability, interlinked to my crude reality.
No man can deny what is clear to see—
This one is too much to bear; this one might be the death of me.

Nakba

You named your child Moses,
yet he did not part the sea.
This is not affirmation ideology.
The staff was not bestowed upon him,
and still he snatched Muhammad's
domains,
sentenced to the Sheol.

The good Samaritan leads by example,
so, tell him, what glory will be restored?
Is the murderer laureled alongside the
monarch?
Is he designated chieftain?

Your envoy is no messenger;
provenance has a lot to say.
To the east, the shrewd bade you to listen.
Nakba means catastrophe;
it marks the confiscation of the terrestrial
by means of fabrication with a modicum of
constancy.

The cup of qahwa still hot on the table, the
jarrah balanced on the tanned one's head—
this is how they left.

Lift the veil of blindness.
Clear your myopic sight before your womb
is pruned to a pulp.

The cobwebs are decorative, delusive.
The tomb is empty; brush off the dust.
Soon enough, the Jerusalemites will return
to their posts.

Grace Rodriguez is a Puerto Rican writer and poet residing in New Jersey, USA. She works as an interpreter and aspires to share her passion for poetry and fantasy through her writing.

www.ingramcontent.com/pod-product-compliance
Lightning Source LLC
LaVergne TN
LVHW041229080426
835508LV00011B/1125